GW01418557

ISBN 978-1-331-77547-8
PIBN 10233136

1 MONTH OF
FREE
READING

at

www.ForgottenBooks.com

---◇---

By purchasing this book you are eligible for one month membership to ForgottenBooks.com, giving you unlimited access to our entire collection of over 1,000,000 titles via our web site and mobile apps.

To claim your free month visit:

www.forgottenbooks.com/free233136

English
Français
Deutsche
Italiano
Español
Português

www.forgottenbooks.com

Mythology Photography **Fiction**
Fishing Christianity **Art** Cooking
Essays Buddhism Freemasonry
Medicine **Biology** Music **Ancient
Egypt** Evolution Carpentry Physics
Dance Geology **Mathematics** Fitness
Shakespeare **Folklore** Yoga Marketing
Confidence Immortality Biographies
Poetry **Psychology** Witchcraft
Electronics Chemistry History **Law**
Accounting **Philosophy** Anthropology
Alchemy Drama Quantum Mechanics
Atheism Sexual Health **Ancient History**
Entrepreneurship Languages Sport
Paleontology Needlework Islam
Metaphysics Investment Archaeology
Parenting Statistics Criminology
Motivational

"AS it fit that I should infuse a bunch of myrrh into the festival goblet, and after the Egyptian manner serve up a dead man's bones at the feast ? I will only show it, and take it away again, and it will make the wine bitter but wholesome. Those married pairs that live as remembering that they must part again, shall at the day of their death be admitted to glorious espousals "—

JEREMY TAYLOR.

◁▷

"GIVE my kindest love to my dear wife, and tell her that the uncommon union, which has so long subsisted between us, has been of such a nature, as I trust is spiritual, and therefore will continue forever and I hope she will be supported under so great a trial, and submit cheerfully to the will of God."—

PRESIDENT EDWARDS' LAST MESSAGE TO HIS WIFE

With His Permission,

Dedicated

To the Honorable Secretary Hay,

Historian, Statesman, Diplomat,

Poet, Friend.

Index to Illustrations.

Esther Burr's Journal

Northampton, Feb. 13, 1741.

THIS is my ninth birthday, and Mrs. Edwards, my mother, has had me stitch these sundry sheets of paper into a book to make me a journal. Methinks, almost all this family keep journals; though they seldom show them. But Mrs. Edwards is to see mine, because she needs to know whether I improve in composing; also, whether I am learning to keep my heart with all diligence; in which we are all constrained to be engaged.

There has been a great religious awakening here among the children. One of my little mates, Phœbe Bartlett, only a few years older than myself, seems to be a wonderful Christian, and has been one, ever since she was four years of age. So Mr. Edwards, my father, thinks. I do not expect to be

head at us and puts her finger on her
lips, but we are sometimes ready to burst
out with mischief: not because he pro=
vokes or deserves it, but because it is in
us; as I venture to say, it is in all
girls.   ❧   ❧   ❧   ❧   ❧   ❧   ❧

Northampton, Jan. 9, 1742.

MRS. Edwards was thirty-three years old to-day. That seems very old. I wonder if I shall live to be thirty-three? And Mr. Edwards is forty—seven years older than she. Mrs. Edwards seemed very serious all the day long; as if she were inwardly praying, "Lord, so teach me to number my days, that I may apply my heart unto wisdom." Indeed, this she said to us girls, when we were trying to practice some birthday frolics upon her. And when she came from her closet-devotions, her face actually shone, as though, like Moses, she had come down from the mount. I do not think we girls ever will be so saintly as our mother is. At any rate, we do not begin so. I do not know as I want to be, which is very wicked, I am sure. I think, that perhaps Sarah may; she is the flower of this family.

Northampton, Jan. 27, 1742.

A flaming young preacher, just from the college at New Haven, has come to town. He preaches, every day, and twice a day; our dear honored father, who so much bears the burdens of all the churches, being absent, doing the work of an evangelist. My precious mother, though she would gladly conceal it, is not a little exercised to see the people flocking after the young herald of the Cross, as though they never heard preaching before. His name is Buell, and he is a classmate in college of Samuel Hopkins. But, I can see this morning that she has wrestled with the Lord, and gotten the victory, for she says so sweetly and triumphantly: "Would God, that all the Lord's people were prophets, and that God would put his spirit upon them." ◦ ◦ ◦ ◦

Mr. Buell will stay the second week, and then Mr. Hopkins will go with him, as a kind of armor-bearer, or lieutenant, to Boston, to capture that city for the Lord. Many Christians have been greatly quickened and sinners converted. I am not certain how my honored father would regard some things that Mr. Buell does. But I am sure, he would say, "The Lord save by whom he will save." ◦ ◦ ◦

Northampton, Jan. 27, again.

WE have just come in from the three o'clock lecture. The place was too strait for us, and the people were deeply moved. Many wept, and not a few remained for a period of three hours for conversation and inquiry. My honored mother, whose spirit answers so quickly to spiritual things, seemed to come back home, "walking and leaping and praising God." As she entered the door, she had my hand, and was singing, not loudly, but as if it were in an inward ecstasy,

"Hosanna to King David's son,
Who reigns on a superior throne!"

All the evening there was something seraphic in her expression, and when she kissed me for the night, methought I looked on the face of an angel. My honored father and dear mother seem to me different from other people in this, that their whole nature is attuned to God's service and praise. They utter themselves at once, as though they felt, if they held their peace, the very stones would cry out. Who knows but they would? the Northampton stones are wont to hear such preaching. 🞛 🞛

Northampton, Feb. 13, 1742.

I have just come tripping up stairs from morning worship, and the song of the service still follows me. I have been thinking what a singing family the Edwards family is. Mother's voice we have heard in psalms and hymns and spiritual songs, ever since our early babyhood. She sang us on our pilgrim way, when we were in our cradles. And to all the house, her voice is always uplifting like the lark's, as though her soul were mounting up to heaven's shining gate on wings of song. If father ever gets low-spirited from his "humors," as he calls them, her voice is to him like medicine, as David's harp was to King Saul. And when she once begins, there is Sarah and Jerusha and myself, like the ascending pipes of an organ, ready to unite in making a joyful noise to the Lord, all over the house so that our home is more like an aviary than the dwelling of a Colonial parson.

Mother has been correcting the few pages of my journal and father has given me to transcribe into it, a description which he wrote of a certain lady, when she was but thirteen years old. This is only three years older than I am now. Here is the extract:—

"They say there is a young lady in New Haven who has a strange sweetness in her mind, and a singular purity in her affections; is most just and conscientious in all conduct, and you could not persuade her to do anything wrong or sinful, if you should give her all the world. She is of a wonderful sweetness and calmness, and universal benevolence of mind; especially, after the great God has manifested himself to her mind. She will sometimes go about from place to place singing sweetly, and seeming to be always full of joy and pleasure, and no one knows for what. She loves to be alone, and walking in the fields and groves, and seems to have some One invisible conversing with her."

This was Sarah Pierrepoint, my precious mother. Mr. Edwards wants me to be like her. What do they say of a young lady, also a minister's daughter, who lives in this town of Northampton? My mother says, My Journal thus far is rather stilted and mature for me; though everything in the family is mature. I have a letter of my father's written when he was younger than I am, which I shall trans-

eribe, just to show where the present
writer gets her stilts and maturity :
To Miss Mary Edwards at Hadley.

Windsor, May 10, 1716.

Dear Sister:—

Through the wonderful good=
ness and mercy of God, there has been
in this place a remarkable outpouring
of the Spirit of God. It still continues,
but I think I have reason to think it is in
some measure diminished; yet, I hope
not much. Three have joined the
church, since you last heard, five now
stand propounded for admission; and I
think about thirty persons come com=
monly on Mondays to converse with
father about the condition of their souls.
It is a time of general health here.
Abigail, Hannah and Lucy have had the
chicken=pox and have recovered. Je=
rusha is almost well. Except her, the
whole family is well.

Sister, I am glad I hear of your
welfare as often as I do. I should be
glad to hear from you by letter, and
therein, how is it with you, as to your
crookedness.

Your loving brother,

Jonathan E.

Northampton, March 6, 1742.

HAVE just been caring for my mocking-bird, who is now rewarding me with a song. The cat was lurking in the hall, and I have just driven her away with the broom, with which I have been sweeping the living-room. Though down by the fireside, at twilight, she is my favorite, too, or rather, Jerusha's, who is very tender of pets. And even father, sometimes, while with us after supper, seems to enjoy her purring, as he strokes her in his lap. Though I doubt if she has much divinity about her; unless it is in her sparks of electricity, when she is rubbed the wrong way.   e   e   e   e   e   e

Northampton, May 1, 1742.

I have just come back from a most wonderful ride with my honored father, Mr. Edwards, through the spring woods. He usually rides alone. But, to-day, he said he had something he wanted to show me. The forests between our house and the full-banked river were very beautiful. The wild cherry and the dogwood were in full bloom. The squirrels were leaping from tree to tree, and the birds were making a various melody. Though father is usually taciturn or preoccupied,—my mother will call these large words,—even when he takes one of us children with him, to-day, he discoursed to me of the awful sweetness of walking with God in Nature. He seems to feel God in the woods, the sky, the clouds and the grand sweep of the river, which winds so majestically through the woody silences here. He quoted, to-day, from the Canticles, "I am the Rose of Sharon and the Lily of the valleys," applying the words to the Saviour, as though the beauty and loveliness of the Saviour were recalled in the works of creation;

and then, from the Gospel of John: "All things were made by him, and without him was not anything made, that was made." This was, as I sat behind on the pillion, which we so much use as a seat for another in horseback riding.   ๏   ๏   ๏   ๏   ๏   ๏

When we reached "The Indian's Well," I slid off and brought a birch-bark cup of crystal water for father to drink.   But, not before I had given myself a great surprise.   For, having put on my mother's hat in sport, the first reflection in the dark water seemed to be the face of my mother instead of my own.   And when I told my father, he said: "As face answereth to face in water, so the heart of man to man." And then he told me, that he had given me that extract about Sarah Pierrepoint, that I might think of what my mother was already, when she was still a young maiden.   ๏   ๏   ๏   ๏

Going home, my father pointed out to me the habits of a flying spider, that sallies forth on his thread as upon wings, and is borne by the wind from tree to tree, so that he really is a great traveler: how he raises himself on tiptoe, turning up his body, how the silk fluid in his body becomes hardened on exposure to the air, how it is drawn out by the current of the air. Indeed, I came home thinking a great many new thoughts, which my excursion had awakened ; as I think my father intend=ed. And the verse came into my mind: "All thy works praise thee!"

Northampton, June, 1743.

MY mother has just come into the house, with a bunch of sweet peas, and put them on the stand where my honored father is shaving, though his beard is very slight. We have abundance of flowers, and a vegetable garden, which is early and thrifty. Our sweet corn is the first in the town, and so are our green peas. My honored father of course has not time to give attention to the garden, and so Mrs. Edwards looks after everything there. Almost before the snow has left the hills, she has it ploughed and spaded by Rose's husband, who does all the hard work there. She is our colored cook. We hire her services from one of the prominent people in father's parish, who owns both her and her husband. That word "owns" sounds strangely about people. * * * * *

Rev. Samuel Hopkins, my father's student in theology, has some very strong opinions against slavery. He once said to my father, that he believed

God would yet overrule for his glory, the coming of the blacks to this country; quoting what Joseph said, "Ye meant it for evil, but God meant it for good." He has already working in his great mind, the beginning of an effort to send Christianized negroes back to Africa. We girls have changed his nickname to "Old Benevolence;" though we all have for him the greatest respect. But, we must have something to make sport about among ourselves.   ❦   ❦   ❦

Northampton, July 23, 1743.

THE Rev. Samuel Hopkins has just paid us a short visit. A very strong attachment has sprung up between this young preacher and my honored father. Indeed, I believe, he has made my father and mother his confidants in a certain affair of the heart, which relates to himself. A certain young lady in Northampton—none of the Edwards girls—is the object of this attachment, and alas, it is not successful. It gives us girls a great theme. ❦ ❦ ❦

Mr. Hopkins was to spend the Lord's Day with us, and to preach in my father's stead; though I really believe he would much prefer to listen to my father. As it turned out, they both preached, and Mr. Hopkins said the comparison made him ashamed.

Northampton, Sept. 14, 1743.

MR. David Brainerd should have graduated at New Haven College this day. Mr. Edwards, my father, is feeling much hurt because President Glap and the Trustees have treated Mr. Brainerd so shabbily and cruelly. My father says, as I think, New Haven College has lost the brightest jewel she will ever wear in her crown. Mr. Brainerd was expelled from the College, for saying of one of the tutors who seemed indifferent to religious activity,—when Mr. Whitefield was preaching in New Haven, and the students were generally giving much attention to his word,—that he had no more religion than a chair. I can see that my father thinks that he spake unadvisedly, and should make amends for it,—as he was willing most humbly to do,—but, that he very likely spoke the truth. Being a graduate of that College, my father has been greatly burdened at the irreligion and wickedness prevailing there; and he is already in conference with Rev. Burr of Newark as to founding a college, perhaps, in the Jerseys, where young men can be safe from such influences.

It seems that Mr. Brainerd was so concerned for the students, that he went from room to room talking and praying with them all, whether they had made a profession of faith or not. Indeed, Mr. Samuel Hopkins told my father that it was David Brainerd's visit to his room that convinced him that he himself was not a Christian, though he was even then intending to study for the ministry.

Northampton, Sept. 14, 1743.

AS I said, to return to the topic above: this day David Brainerd would have graduated at New Haven College. But, the Faculty were unrelenting, notwithstanding his humiliating confession. He is likely to become a member of this family, it seems. Soon after coming to Northampton he displayed strong affinity for Jerusha, our sister of seventeen, who was soon inoculated with his high spiritual views, and deeply interested in his Indian work.

My honored father Mr. Edwards regards him a young man of uncommon abilities and gifts of nature, a close student, with extraordinary power in the pulpit. In private conversation, he is entertaining and profitable, and very instructive on personal and experimental religion. Thus far, his Indian Missionary labors have been solitary. He thinks this a mistake. He has had no domestic attention, no home care, no one to hold him back from over exertion. And he means now, should he ever recover, which I very much misdoubt; to take a female helpmate back with him. I am pretty sure this kind of

love never would satisfy me. I believe
he loves her, more because she will
make a good missionary, than for any
other reason. But, little does the dear
girl care. She has laid herself upon the
altar, and is more than willing to be an
offering for a sweet smelling savour to
him, as well as to her divine saviour
and Lord.

Northampton, May 14, 1744.

MRS. Edwards, my mother, and my sister Sarah have just set out with Mr. Hopkins on horseback for Boston. My sister rides behind Mr. Hopkins, and they are to lodge the first night at Colonel Dwight's in Brookfield. This leaves a great vacancy in our busy home: and intent on his studies as my honored father Mr. Edwards is, I really believe he feels it the most. This visit to Boston has been a long time planned, to execute sundry purchases needful for the members of the household. While in Boston, mother and Sarah are to be entertained at the house of Rev. Mr. Prince. Mr. Prince has a daughter Sally, younger than our Sarah—father does not like to hear her nick-named—with whom, I sometimes exchange letters. I hope hereafter to visit Boston, myself; though I believe, I would rather reside in Northampton.

Northampton, Feb. 14, 1747.

I think I never knew so hapyy a day. There has been a thaw, the January thaw, later than usual, and the rain had frozen on every tree and twig, and when the sun arose, it was just as though they were all encased in silver. And everywhere the broken pieces of ice were crackling down from the elms and maples, all the way as we went to the house of God. The air was full of music of the sleigh-bells of the church-goers, as they drove past. And I thought of what is said in the Scriptures, of the bells on the high priest's garments, and how his sound was heard as he went into the holy place; and so the greater music of the church-bells seemed to say to my soul, holiness to the Lord!

But I must begin to speak of earlier in the day. I was awkened in the morning by someone's kissing me on my eyes and my mouth and my ears. In the haze of my morning dreams I thought it might be the angels. But, no, I soon saw that it was my angel-mother,

and she was half saying and half singing: "Awake, my Esther, my queen.
This is the day of thine espousals. For
the King delighteth in thee and calleth
thee by name. He brings thee to His
banqueting-house and His banner over
thee is love." Then, I remembered it
was my fifteenth birthday, and also,
that I was that day, to take upon me the
vows of God. And I answered mother,
as by a kind of inspiration: "I was
asleep, but my heart waketh. It is the
voice of my beloved that knocketh. His
head is filled with dew, His locks with
the drops of the night." And I quickly
arose, for I saw the house was already
astir. ❦ ❦ ❦ ❦ ❦ ❦ ❦

My honored father preached on
Ruth's Resolution as though to me,
from the words, "Entreat me not to
leave thee, nor to turn from following
thee." (Ruth i, 16.) I shall never forget
his words about the people of God. He
said, "They are the most excellent and
happy society in the world. God whom
they have chosen as their God, is their
Father. He has pardoned all their sins,
and they are at peace with Him. And
He has admitted them to all the privil-
eges of children. As they have devoted

themselves to God, so God has given Himself to them. He carries them on eagle's wings far above Satan's reach, and above the reach of all their enemies in this world." This he afterwards let me copy from his sermon. And I said in my heart: "Thy people shall be my people, and thy God my God."   &   &

Northampton, 1747.

JERUSHA has just returned from her sojourn in Boston, with her sick charge, David Brainerd, the Indian Missionary. They came by easy stages, but he is much exhausted, and I believe, is not long for this world. Never was there such devotion, shall I say idolatry? bestowed upon mortal man. Never was there so humble a handmaid of the Lord as Jerusha. She reminds me of what is said of Ruth and Boaz: "When she fell upon her face and bowed herself to the ground, and said unto him, Why have I found grace in thy sight, that thou shouldst take knowledge of me?" Her whole nature goes out after spiritual things, and this man is her ideal. She actually almost worships the ground he treads upon. She feels that she is unworthy to perform the most menial offices for him. She is just sure to wear herself out in her constant ministrations, which are day and night, unremitting and unceasing. If he should die soon, and I believe he will, I am sure she would prefer to die with him, as Thomas said to the Lord about Lazarus, "Let us go that we may die with him!'' Indeed, we all fear, that with the close of his life, she will feel that her work is ended, like Simeon saying, "Now lettest thy servant depart in peace.''

Northamton, Oct. 9, 1747.

THE sainted sufferer of the house, our temporary guest, our brother in the Lord, has at length, breathed his last. He called us all to his bedside, and tenderly talked of his going, and bade us, when we stand by his grave, to remember his words. He expressed himself ready to part with us all. "For to depart and be with Christ was far better." To our Jerusha, his long=time nurse, who has watched and almost felt every pang of his poor rack= ed body, for many months, he said: "Dear Jerusha, are you willing to part with me? I am quite willing to part with you. Though if I thought I should not see you and be happy with you in another world, I could not bear to part with you. But, we will spend a happy eternity together." And so he had his message for each one of us all, and then fell asleep.

Northamton, Oct. 12, 1747.

WE have just come home from the public improvement of David Brainerd's decease. Of course, my honored father preached the discourse. His text was from 2 Cor. v. 8 : "Absent from the body but present with the Lord."

He was unusually exalted, even for him. The closing hymn was
"Why do we mourn departed friends?
"Or shrink at death's alarms?"
It was sung grandly and triumphantly by our great choir of voices. Dear Jerusha's illuminated face was a study. She was rapt up no more in the living. It seemed as though her soul, liberated from earth, was already mounting up to holy communion with the spirits of the just made perfect, of whom not one of the great congregation could doubt, Mr. Branerd was now one. And when came the words

"Are we not tending upward too,
As fast as time can move?
Nor would we wish the hours more
slow
To keep us from our love!"

it seemed to me as though she saw
heaven open, the golden gates lifted
up and was only waiting for angel-
wings to mount there. She is not long
for this world. For exactly nineteen
weeks, day and night, she has cared
for this sick man ; and she only eight=
een. ℮ ℮ ℮ ℮ ℮ ℮

⚜ ⚜

Northampton, Oct. 12, 1747.

MUCH respect was shown Mr. Brainerd's memory at the funeral, which occurred to-day: eight of the neighboring ministers being present, seventeen gentlemen of liberal education and a great concourse of people. The October foliage, full of glory, seemed Nature's expression of the triumphal conclusion of his life's years; and when we all stood at the open grave, and his precious dust was committed to the dust, my father pronouncing the words: "And I heard a voice from heaven saying, 'Blessed are the dead that die in the Lord;' yea, saith with the Spirit that they may rest from their labors, and their works do follow them," it was a solemnity not soon to be forgotten. And when we returned home to the dwelling where he had suffered so long, it was like coming back to earth from the gateway of Heaven. How strangely earth and Heaven are brought together in this family! ❧ ❧ ❧ ❧ ❧ ❧ ❧

Northampton, 1747.

MY honored father has not only thought it a sacred duty to care for Mr. Brainerd in his own house, as a friend and guest, remembering the words, "Be not forgetful to entertain strangers; for by so doing, many have entertained angels unawares:" but he has felt that a record of his saintly exercises and experiences should be made for others. He firmly believes that the journal he has kept, is to be largely blessed in making ministers and missionaries, till the end of time. ❧ ❧ ❧ ❧ ❧ ❧ ❧

Northampton, Feb. 14, 1748.

THIS day our dear Jerusha died at eighteen. If as she and her sainted David, and we all believe, she be gone to her Father's House, she has already joined the holy company, of which he since last October has been one. They have been separated only five months. Though I doubt, whether he has ever been absent from her thought and longing love. This is what the world calls St. Valentine's day, though I have been taught to think that all folly. Being a girl, I suppose, I could not help remarking the coincidence. And I recalled from the Psalms as it was my day's reading: "She shall be brought unto the King, in raiment of needle-work; the virgins, her companions, that follow her shall be brought unto thee; they shall enter into the King's palace." And so we shall lay the frame of this ministering angel side by side with that of the man, who breathed out his life almost in her arms. It is just five months and two days since his burial. Now they can say in concert, "My beloved is mine, and I am His!"

II

Northampton, January.

GREAT excitement has been occasioned by a New Year's sleigh-ride and ball for dancing, that has just occurred here. It was a gay party of young people, some of my more intimate friends among them, who drove to a hotel in Hadley, and spent the hours till midnight in dancing the Old Year out and the New Year in. When it was known such a party was in contemplation, the mothers of the young people had a prayer-meeting to pray that no harm might come to them ; indeed, that they might be converted to a better style of piety, than they then had; for many of them were already church-members. To my honored father and mother, it has been a time of great grief. And when with morning light, the great sledloads drove up through the streets, with their laughing, giddy freight, I saw the tears in the eyes of them both. I am only too glad, that none of the children of this family were invited to go: or had they been, would have so far departed from the wishes of their parents, as to care to do so. This household, even when there are visiting young people as guests, is so well regulated, that with nine o'clock comes the hour for family worship when the different members retire; while our morning worship is usually by candlelight.   ●   ●   ●   ●

Northampton.

WE have just been permitted
to read Richardson's nov=
el: "Sir Charles Grandi=
son." Our father and moth=
er have first read it, and
regard it a wholly suitable book as to
morals and character. Our honored fa=
ther has gone so far as to express ad=
miration for its literary style, and also
to speak his regret that he had not ear=
lier given more attention to such mat=
ters; he being so intent upon the
thougt, as to have no time to clothe it
in elegant language. This novel was
sent to us from Scotland, where it had
made a great stir. Of course, to read
such a book, is an unusual event in such
a family as ours. And we have had a
great time taking it in turn, and discus=
sing its characters.   ℮   ℮   ℮   ℮

Northampton.

THIS day, we leave dear, sweet Northampton, where all of us have been born, and where we have so many ties of childhood and youth. Even the very trees around our home, seem a part of us. There is one elm, that is called my father's, he has so long studied beneath it. Though these places will know us no more forever, though much bitterness and persecution have marked the men who have compassed our departure, as my honored father says, we do not go as David left Jerusalem driven out by the rebellion of his son Absalom,—though it seems so to me at least,—but believing in the words of the sacred writ: "Behold, I send an angel before thee, to bring thee into the place which I have prepared. Lead me in thy righteousness because of mine enemies; make thy way straight before my face." ⚬ ⚬ ⚬ ⚬ ⚬

One of the bitterest experiences connected with this removal is the fact that some of the active instigators of it are actually flesh of our flesh, and blood of our blood. This is more than the Psalmist's complaint of the one who "lifted up the heel against him:" "We took sweet counsel together, and walked to the house of God in company," though this also was true. And doubtless, the Lord's servants have to take the baptism of their Master, who quotes this passage with reference to the defection of Judas.

Northampton.

NOTHING could be more beautiful than the manner, in which Mr. and Mrs. Edwards have submitted to the decision of the Council with its majority of only one, recommending our removal from this place. We children have been indignant beyond expression. It has not always been possible for us to please our parents by showing a meek and quiet spirit. And seeing them take everything so patiently, we have sometimes seemed to feel the more satisfaction in showing our resentment. May God forgive us, if we are wrong. But we feel like shaking the dust off of our very feet, as a testimony against a people, to whom our father has ministered in holy things for so many years, and who have been born of his ministration of the truth into the Kingdom of God.

Stockbridge, Mass., Dec. 22, 1748.

A letter to Mr. Edwards, my honored father, from Mr. Burr, states that the New Jersey College was organized under an enlarged charter, Nov. 9, and that he has been chosen President to succeed Mr. Dickenson, who has lately died. For the present, he will serve without salary. There is a graduating class of eight, of whom seven expect to be ministers of the Gospel. Mr. Burr has two tutors to assist him. He himself teaches the ancient languages and mathematics, calculates eclipses and practices surveying, besides being the pastor of the church there. But of work, my honored father says, Mr. Burr never tires, and he passes from one thing to another, with the greatest facility and grace. This whole arrangement, which has been discussed in a correspondence between my father and Governor Belcher is very satisfactory. It is not anticipated that Mr. Burr will resign his pastorate, at least, at present; though how he finds time to do so much none of us can guess.

Stockbridge, May 26, 1749.

IT is the practice of Mr. Edwards to finish his own meal, which is always very simple, and then return to the table to say grace, at the close, when we are all done. For we begin and end our meals in God. This morning as he did not come at once, my dear mother who always herself says grace, when father is absent from home, said that Jonathan Edwards, Jr., who is just past eight years old, might officiate. This pleased us all. For he fell into father's exact words and intonations, as a child would do, without seeming to intend it. We all maintained the greatest decorum, as was befitting, for we know that "out of the mouth of babes and sucklings God has ordained praise"—a favorite verse of father's, who believes in the early conversion of children. This evening, too, we children are to have a birthday festival in Jonathan's honor, though this we keep a profound secret. As to Jonathan, Jr., we all expect he will some day make a great divine; though outwardly he does not resemble our father; being dark, and plain, and very small.   &   &

Stockbridge, Jan. 21, 1752.

THIS town is delightfully located for winter sports. The river has a very quiet flow, so that we have skating parties, and the hills all around furnish suitable declivities for coasting. I have just come in from West Stockbridge road, with my cheeks all aglow and pulse beating wildly. My sister and I had two Indian boys to pull our sleds for us, and to guide them over the crust, which flashes like a mirror, as with lightning rapidity we speed from one descent to another, until we finally reach the level of our quiet street. At the corners, the wood men came in with their heavily loaded wood-sleds, and the sleigh bells rang right merrily as though it were a winter's holiday.

Stockbridge, Jan. 27, 1752.

THE sacred writer said, "O that I had wings like a dove, that I might fly away, and be at rest." Even Stockbridge has my honored father's enemies. Not Indians, that lurk in the wilderness and waylay the unsuspecting victim. Our Indians, especially the Housatonacs, are peaceable and docile. There is not a member of this family, that is not engaged in giving them instruction in the Bible. And our honored father has determined to send Jonathan the second when he is nine years old to live among Mr. Brainerd's Indians, that he may learn their language in his childhood, and thus escape the hard labor of acquiring a language in his adult life. Not Indians, but the scattered remnants of that bitter company, who moved my father from Northampton.

My father has just written to his own father: "My wife and children are well pleased with our present situation. They like the place far better than they expected. Here, at present, we live in peace; which has, of a long time, been unusual to us. The Indians seem much pleased with our family, especially my wife." And yet, there is trouble enough here. It was only the other day, that a visitor to the male Mohawk school struck a child of the Chief Sachem of the Onoquagas on the head with his cane, without any provocation. The Iroquois are all indignant, and threaten to leave the town. Very improper use has been made of the moneys which have been sent here by Mr. Hollis, the English patron of the Indian schools. The individual who has received these moneys, has had no school established, and kept no regular account of his expenditures. The Indian children have been permitted to grow up in filth and ignorance. But as this man has married into the family of the resident trustee all of this is covered up. But, of course, Mr. Edwards feels bound in duty, to communicate the facts to the Boston Commissioners.   ❧   ❧   ❧

Stockbridge, Feb. 2, 1752.

ISS Salty Prince of Boston, whose father is a great friend of my father's, and who is herself a great friend of mine, has been writing me about the sports of the winter in that city. With us simple country people, the chief place of social recreation and amusement is the singing-school. Besides the pleasure of getting together one evening each week, when we are arranged for part singing, the singers are permitted to sit in the gallery on Sundays, if they promise to keep to their own seats, and not infringe on the women's pews. The women, of course, do not need to make any such promise about the men. Sometimes, indeed, we have sleighing parties, and those that love dancing finish up such parties with a social dance. Though my honored father believes that such customs are full of danger to young people. In that sermon at Northampton, which created the great disturbance, resulting in his being dismissed, I remember he said this: "I do not desire that young people should be abridged of any proper liberties," showing that he was

not arbitrary and unreasonable in his
views: but that certain social practices
were creeping in that deserved his re-
buke.   ❧   ❧   ❧   ❧   ❧   ❧   ❧

Stockbridge, Feb., 1725.

HIS family is very busy making lace and embroidery, so as to replenish the household treasury. In Northampton, my honored father had purchased a valuable homestead, with land for fuel and pasturing, and had erected a commodious dwelling house. These had, by our exercising the strictest economy, all been paid for, before his removal. Among the bitterest of our experiences, therefore, was to be sent roofless and homeless to a wilderness. But, neither my honored mother, nor any of the children bated a jot of hope. We began at once, the making and decoration of fans and other ornamental work, which we were assisted to dispose of in Boston, by our friends the Princes there. How narrow our circumstances were, may be seen from the necessity put upon our father, to use the margins of otherwise useless pamphlets and the backs of letters, on which to write his sermons and treaties. But, he knows no other law of life, and so he

keeps on with his thirteen hours a day
in his study.   He has lately had a hex=
agonal table made, with six several in=
clining leaves, so that he can have his
books of reference before his eyes, all
at once, and can leave them open at the
passage where he leaves off.   ⅇ   ⅇ

Stockbridge.

A NEW sound echoes through our hills. Every Sabbath day, and every lecture-day, one of the praying Indians blows a conch-shell, to call the people to worship. At first, it seemed wanting in solemnity, but, now we are used to it, the shell begins to have a sacred sound, and the summons is speedily heeded. I am fond of watching the people as they congregate: The Indians gliding up the river-bank in their noiseless canoes, the farmers and wives on horseback, with children in arms, or tucked in, here and there, as there is space for them, the pedestrians: rich and poor meeting together before the Lord, who is Maker of us all.

1725

Stockbridge, May, 1752.

THIS has just happened to me: Rev. Mr. Burr of Newark, President of the New Jersey College, who has visited our house, both in Northampton and Stockbridge for many years;—as a little girl, I have romped with him, and sat on his lap, rose this A. M. to take an early breakfast and start for home again, betimes, on horseback to the Hudson. And as it was my week to care for the table, I had spread the breakfast for him, no other member of the family having yet arisen. The cloth was as white as snow, for I had taken out a fresh one with its clean smell, for the occasion, and there was not a crease in it; the room was full of the aroma of the freshly made tea. I had selected some of the last caddy, that came from the Rev. Thomas Prince's of Boston, a family very dear to us. The newly churned butter was as yellow as gold. I had rolled it and stamped it with my own hands. And to top the whole, one of our father's deacons, an Indian, who knew of Mr. Burr's early start, had brought in some fish freshly taken from the Housatonic. Mr. Burr

partook with the greatest relish, keeping up a current of gracious speech, every moment; and finally fixing his
flashing eyes on me, as I sat rapt and
listening at the other end of the board,
he abruptly said: "Esther Edwards,
last night, I made bold to ask your honored father, if I can gain your consent,
that I might take you as Mrs. Burr, to
my Newark bachelor's quarters and
help convert them into a Christian
home. What say you?" Of course, although from my early girlhood, Mr.
Burr had treated me with favor, I was
wholly unprepared for this sudden
speech, and blushed to my ears and
looked down; and stammered out, as
we are taught to say here: "If it please
the Lord!" Though when we came to
separate, I could not help playfully saying, "Was it the loaves and fishes, Mr.
Burr?" He laughed, and kissed me for
the first time.   ❦   ❦   ❦   ❦   ❦

I am only seventeen, and I had never received such attention from any person. And it has set my being all aglow
with new life. And so we parted, he for
his ride through the wilderness to the

Hudson, and I to resume my domestic
duties. I soon heard my heart keeping
time to his horse's hoofs as they made
the turnpike echo, and I paused to
watch the splendid animal ascend the
hillside to the West. The sun was just
rising, and smiting the river mists with
its rod of gold. And I went about all
day, making melody in my heart to the
Lord. My dear mother appeared to sur=
mise the new secret of my life for,
doubtless, Mr. Edwards had told her,
as they have no secrets from each other,
but said nothing. Meanwhile, I tried to
imagine Mr. Burr's progress from point
to point, until he reach=d the sloop on
the river, and then I seemed to lose him
among the highlands, as the sloop bore
him seaward to Newark, my heart with
him. I could not help asking myself:
"Has he been waiting for me, all these
years?" At any rate, I thought to my=
self, I am his Rachel; his lamb, as the
word means. Nor do I need to steal my
father's gods, as did she. For already
his God is my God! and his people,
my people.   e   e   e   e   e   e

Stockbridge, March, 1752.

THE pressure of duties upon Mr. Edwards, my honored father, has been so great, that it seems almost impossible for him to endure it. What with preaching to the white people, and the Indians, and catechising the children: what with putting up a new dwelling-house and getting together money to pay for it: what with the intrigues of those who are secretly obstructing his work and trying to supplant him; and what with his constant thinking and writing, my honored mother is fearful that his health will be utterly broken down. Indeed, he already has the symptoms of ague and fever, which is very prevalent in these new settlements. ❧ ❧ ❧ ❧ ❧

Stockbridge, June 8, 1752.

THIS is my last day in Stockbridge, in this dear home, with my honored mother and sisters. The orchards are filled with apple=bloom as for a bridal. Dear beautiful Stockbridge; the sweetest place on earth, with her mountains tree=topped to the blue skies, her miniature meadows along the Housatonic, where the Indians have their picturesque encampments, the river, willow=embosomed, where the strong arms of my tawny friends have so often noiselessly guided the canoe, and we have glided as in a dream. Yes, also dear sanctuary of God, where the red man and the white man have dwelt together in peace, as in their own Father's House, and where my good father's instruction has so often fallen upon us all alike, as manna from Heaven. "Blessed are they that dwell in thy house; they shall still be praising thee."   ❧   ❧   ❧

Stockbridge.

I HAVE sometimes essayed a description to myself of Mr. Edwards. Let me do it again, before I leave my father's house for the house of my husband. His face is almost womanly in refinement and feature, and grace. There is a kind of sweet sedateness, an elevated, almost celestial serenity, to some, perhaps severity, of expression. And when he is speaking in the pulpit, it often seems that his voice has a supernatural, an angelic tenderness and authority. There is in his utterance no weakness or softness, though it is not a loud voice nor very masculine. There is such a holy loyalty to the truth in the speaker, as though he were one of God's swift messengers, unwinged indeed, save in the spirit, which often tries lofty flights, but coming straight from the ineffable glory, commissioned of infinite love to proclaim the truth and defend it. In person, he sometimes reminds me of Michael Angelo's arch-angel with drawn sword; of pictures of John the

Evangelist, which our Scotland friends, the Erskines, have sent us, and which hang in our living room.   ❧   ❧   ❧

Stockbridge, June, 1752.

THE good man who has chos-
en me for his bride, has sent
a young messenger from
Newark, with two horses, to
conduct my honored mother
and myself to New Jersey. He says,
There is plenty of Scripture for it. Did
not Isaac thus send for Rebekah? I am
to ride Nimrod, Mr. Burr's great admir-
ation and pride. I am glad to go. I
suppose I feel some as did Christiana,
in "Pilgrim's Progress," when she had
summons to follow her husband. Is it
wrong to think of my new home as the
type of heaven? I hope it is not wrong
to feel so. I had to kiss the bark of the
elm=tree, that stands in front of my window, and where I have so often watched
the returning robins, as they built their
nests and reared their young, and then
taught them to fly away; and now I am
to stretch my wings and go, after their
example. But, mine are the wings of
the dove!   *   *   *   *   *   *

When we mounted the hill, on our
way toward West Stockbridge, I was
fain to turn again and look back on the
lovely little town in the valley, and the
surrounding mountains in their grand=

eur.   On either side stood the hills, late=
ly clothed with new verdure; between
them, the beautiful intervales, beneath
which crept the river, the smooth=glid=
ing Housatonic, and where were feeding
the cattle.   I shut my eyes if I might fix
the picture and make it mine forever,
and then rode on with my companions.
And soon Nimrod, with his eager spirit,
gave me enough to attend to.   He seem=
ed to know he was taking me to his
master.   &   &   &   &   &   &

We took the turnpike to the Hud=
son.   The road having been lately
mended, our progress was slow.   In=
deed, there were some passages where
the men were still at work picking out
the stones and the stumps.   But, even
this gave us all the more leisure to look
at the beautiful woods, and to hear the
brooks full of glancing fish, bubbling
by the roadside.   The birds were very
lively with their songs, and the bushy=
tailed squirrels were full of their
pranks.   The early dews, too, were
dropping on the leaves.   And soon my
steed having come to know his rider,
moved on obediently, and as though
more than satisfied with his burden.
Our riding companion, who has just

graduated at the College, was not very talkative, though quite enough so for me. My dear mother, who was with us —but, ah, only a mother could know the soliloquies going on in her heart. She hid all those mother-thoughts, even from me. I am afraid, it sometimes seemed to her, that she was accompanying her Isaac, to a place that God would tell her of—for the altar.   ❦   ❦   ❦

❦ ❦ ❦

Esther Burr's Song.

My love hath love that he sendeth me
From the piney wild of the Newark sea,
    From the piney wilds, where the mayflow'r blows,
    And the princely Hudson seaward goes
And I have love, that I waft to him,
As I mount my steed for the Hudson's brim,
As I mount my steed and speed to him

On Sloop, Hudson River.

NOW I know what a grand river is. Our own Connecticut at Northampton, as it sweeps along through the wide intervales, especially in the spring time, when its bosom is full, is a very impressive sight: but the scene is still rather picturesque, than grand. There is an attractive softness about the whole landscape. The mountains are distant, and not so high. But, here the mountains crowd up to the very banks of the river, as if to dispute its progress to the sea; as sometimes to the eye, while we move along through their fastnesses, they seem actually to have done. The lights and shadows made upon them by the floating clouds, their own reflection in the water, the great width of the river, sometimes almost like a lake with here and there a Dutch village, or an Indian encampment on either bank, the exhilaration of the whole, I can never forget. And then, when we came to what one might call the palisades, there were new attractions. At length, New York, at the mouth of the river, with its harbor of sloops, and here and there, a larger vessel. And then Newark bay and river, and my new home in the Jerseys.—And, then, taking the trip without Mr. Burr, as it were, added to the romance. It seemed more like realizing the Scripture words respecting marriage: about leaving father and mother. Though mother, bless her sweet heart, is with me still. I could not dream her away; blessed soul!   e   e   e   e   e

Newark, N. J., June 29, 1752.

THIS day I was married to the man who has chosen me for his helpmate in the Lord; and, who, I have reasons to believe has been waiting for me as long as Jacob tarried for Rachel. He is my senior in years, but is young and elastic in spirit, full of Christian enterprise. Though short in stature, compared with my honored father, who is very tall: and though of a delicate frame, like my father, he is all energy and zeal: moving here and there and everywhere, almost like a flash of light. And yet he is modest and unassuming; though everywhere at his ease; courteous too, and obliging to all. He has been pastor here for fifteen years, and he is almost his people's idol. And now I have come to address myself to the duties of a pastor's wife, in which, although I have my mother as an example, I am so unlike her that the task does not seem an easy one. She began her married life at seventeen. I begin mine at 18=19. Mr. Burr has acquired the reputation here, of being a lover of hospitality. His door is always open, and his board always full. He is a bountiful giver, and though himself abstemious at the table, he wants to see it generously furnished, and as he has the means to do it, I shall try to gratify him; though it will be very much better provided than our own table, at my father's house, where evreything was as simple and plain as possible. Though in Northampton and Stockbridge, Mr. and Mrs. Edwards were careful to fulfill the injunction: "Use hospitality without grudging." The stranger was always welcome. ❦ ❦ ❦ ❦ ❦ ❦ ❦

Newark, 1752.

MY husband, Mr. Burr, has persuaded me to take up Latin with him. I had learned it a little in our home at Northampton, where was much teaching of the classics. And last evening he read with me a letter of the Roman orator Cicero, addressed in his exile, "To his Dear Terentia, his Little Tullia, and his Darling Cicero." Mr. Burr believes it to be genuine. Mr. Burr was speaking of Cicero's surprise that great calamity should have overtaken one, whose wife had so faithfully worshipped the gods, and who had himself been so serviceable to man, and said it reminded him of what the Tempter says of the patriarch, "Doth Job serve God for naught?" And then he remarked the effeminate sensibility of the writer, who says he would write oftener, did not writing make his grief at their separation more insupportable; drawing a parallel to their advantage with the words of Job: "Though he slay me, yet will I trust in him!" This is a habit with Mr. Burr. It is as though he carried the two worlds in his mind in that parallel manner.

Newark, 1752.

IT has been a great refreshment to my soul, to-day, to hear again Mr. Edwards, my honored father, from the pulpit. I still think, there is none like him. He was corresponding member of the Presbyterian Synod, which sat here, and he preached from James II:19. It was especially grateful to his daughter to witness, in this strange land, how eagerly his words were received, especially by all of the ministers. There are those in two continents who honor and revere his name, though Northampton, in her worldly pride, cast him out and spat upon him. I never recall that, without thinking of how Absalom and those that felt with him, treated David the King in his exile from his throne. It was Absalom in both cases, a young upstart in his pride, who was most officious. I shall yet live to see how humbly some of those people will return with confession and tears. Though this is not becoming in a minister's daughter and a minister's wife. ❦ ❦ ❦ ❦ ❦ ❦

Newark, 1752.

MR. Burr read to me again from the letters of Cicero to his wife and children. In this letter, as Mr. Burr translated it, occurs this passage: "It is our very virtue, which has brought us disgrace. We have committed no other fault than that of surviving our own good fortune." The great Roman, Mr. Burr said, wonders that virtue should be so maligned and punished. The greater Apostle could write to the elders of the church at Ephesus: "None of these things move me, neither count I my life dear unto me, so that I may finish my course with joy." And a greater than the Apostle has put it among the beatitudes of his kingdom: "Blessed are ye when men shall revile you and persecute you and say all manner of evil against you false= ly for my sake." What a contrast be= tween the triumphant Christian martyr, and the puzzled and discouraged feel= ing of the pagan philosopher. Terentia, as he had said before, had done what she could to appease the gods by her piety, and he to propitiate the people by his service.   But, this combination of religion and morality did not protect them. They did not seem to know, that God's real children are made perfect through suffering. This is the Christian mystery, to which the Master introduces us. ❧ ❧ ❧ ❧ ❧ ❧

Newark, April, 1753.

MR. Burr has just rode up to the door on his Nimrod, the saddle horse, which he had me name Nimrod, because he had been a great hunter—and in which we both of us take much pride. He beckoned to me as I sat at the window with my sewing, and I glided down to pat Nimrod's glossy neck, and to kiss the handsome rider. He has just set out alone for Elizabeth, where once dwelt the Rev. Mr. Dickenson, who was interested with my husband in the founding of the new college, and where is the residence of Governor Belcher. Sometimes our colored man, Harry, who is very conceited about his skill as a horseman, drives Mr. Burr on such trips; but, at this season of the year, the roads are so unsettled, Mr. Burr prefers the saddle. I have come back to my sewing, but I keep the picture of my knight in my mind's eye: the slender but erect figure, the steed champing his bit, with mottled back and sides, and his neck clothed with thunder; the graceful horseman—for I must

come back to him—sitting in the saddle
as though born there; as though horse
and man were but one, according to the
classic conception of the centaur.

Newark, Dec., 1754.

HAVE had a sweet and precious letter from my own dear honored mother, full of sympathy and appreciation. She writes of the sacred privilege of motherhood. Indeed, I have heard her say, that she should be willing to be the mother of children, even if they were to have no protracted life in this world; she has such an exalted conception of their destiny hereafter. "Of such is the Kingdom of God." She cautions me tenderly as to the effect of the feelings and affections of the mother upon the child unborn: and assures me, as myself the daughter of many prayers, that I may safely entrust all my anxieties to a covenant God. This was in answer to a letter in which I had intimated a happy secret, which is gladdening our Newark home. I do not forget that she herself seemed especially to walk with God, when the advent of another member of her own family=circle was drawing nigh. She always seemed to feel that all her children were gotten from the Lord, as the first human mother expresses it.   s

Newark, Jan., 1754.

THE first year of my married life, I often found myself comparing Mr. Burr, my good husband, with Mr. Edwards, my honored father. Having always heard my father preach from my childhood, and knowing that he is reckoned a prince among the Lord's servants, this is not strange. I think my father more impressive and solemn; but, Mr. Burr is more ingratiating, and captivating; has more of what people call eloquence. My honored father has such rigid and intense earnestness, that he is led almost to scorn all adornment of discourse. While of late years, writing on his abstract treatises, and preaching largely to the Indians of Stockbridge, who are but little demonstrative, he has grown more and more careless of outward grace. Besides he is by nature more reserved. Mr. Burr's nature seems to bubble up and overflow into expression, taking on beautiful tinted sprays like the water of a fountain. He often seems

to me less a man commissioned to wit=
ness against the wickedness of a sinful
world, than a celestial messenger of in=
vitation winged to earth, his face radi=
ant, his eyes full of kindly fire and his
voice melody itself. But, every man af=
ter his own order. Since 1738, sixteen
years, beginning with his twenty=third
year, he has been pastor here.   ❧   ❧

Newark, Nov. 25, 1754.

THIS day is the appointed day for our wood carting. The farmers in our parish bring load after load of wood from the parsonage lot, and it is chopped up in the yard and made ready for the fire-place. Such a day of confusion it has been! Such a noise of driving oxen, I hope we may never have for a twelve month at least. ❧ ❧ ❧

Next week, the Presbytery is to sit here, and it is expected they will dismiss Mr. Burr from the church and congregation, to give himself wholly to the care of the College. It is a severe strain upon us all. For here, as I have said before, he is almost idolized. But, he thinks of the demands upon young men, as godly ministers, and we are both willing to make the sacrifice. I can see plainly that it all goes back to successfully founding an institution where young men can be fitted for the Christian ministry; the long dream and prayer of Mr. Edwards as well as of himself. ❧ ❧ ❧ ❧ ❧ ❧

Newark, Dec. 1, 1754.

EXTREMELY hurried preparing for the Presbytery. Tuesday provided a dinner and nobody came until afternoon. Enough to try a body's patience. In the evening they came thick and fast. Presbytery sat on our affairs, and adjourned till January. Our people are in a great pickle. Some of them show a very bad spirit.   e   e   e

Thursday: Dined   ten   ministers. This day, Presbytery examined a young candidate for the ministry for one of the Dutch Islands in the West Indies.   e

Newark, Jan. 1, 1755.

A day set apart for fasting and prayer, on account of the late encroachments of the French, and their designs against the British Colonies of America. President Burr preached what was largely a historical discourse, giving the French progress from the time of Henry IV. These were the closing paragraphs:

"Shall we tamely suffer our delightful possessions to be taken from us? become the dupes and the slaves of a French tyrant? God forbid! 'Tis high time to awake, to call up all the Briton within us, every spark of English valor, cheerfully to offer up our purses, our arms, and our lives to the defence of our country, our holy religion, our excellent constitution, and invaluable liberties. For what is Life without Liberty? 'Tis not worth having. A freeborn Briton should disdain the life of a slave. Better, far better to sacrifice it to the defence of our liberty and country, than to survive the dismal day, when these regions of light and liberty shall be overspread with ignorance, superstition, and tyranny. And had we but the spirit of our brave ancestors, who cheerfully ventured their lives, and resigned all the comforts thereof in an howling wilderness, were we animated by the same heroic spirit in defence of them, with the same ardent desire of leaving them inviolate to posterity, we should soon make our enemies flee before us, and again sit quietly under our own vines and fig-trees, and eat of the good of the land!"

ONDAY, January 12, 1756.— Mr. Burr gone to New York, and I as busy as a bee.

Tuesday Eve.—This eve Miss Sukey, our wench, began with me about her soul's concern. And I find she has had a great many serious thoughts since she has been here. She is full of her inquiries as to what she must do to be good. She tells me she tries to pray from the heart, but finds she can't, and she seems to have some sense of sin. How my heart is rejoiced! O that God would give us this one soul! It seems as if I could not be denied my request, that God would perfect the good work that seems to have begun in her whilst in this house, O how great a blessing upon us! I hope God has heard some of my poor prayers for her. And I hope for a heart to pray more earnestly for her than ever. What a comfort to see those under our care inclining to the ways of religion and true virtue.

March 26, 1756.—I was unexpectedly delivered of a son the 6th of February. Had a fine time, although it pleased God in infinite wisdom to order that

Mr. Burr was not at home. It seemed very gloomy when I found my time had come, to think that I was, as it were, destitute of earthly friends. No mother, no husband, and none of my particular friends that belong to the town; they happening to be out of town. But O my dear God was all these relations and more than all to me in the hour of my distress. Those words in Psalms were my support and comfort through the whole: "They that trust in the Lord shall be as Mt. Zion that cannot be moved, but abideth forever;" and these also, "As the mountains are round about Jerusalem, so is the Lord round about them that trust in him," or words to that purpose.   e   e   e

I had a very quick and good time, a very good lying in till about three weeks, then I had the canker very bad, and before I had recovered of that my little Aaron (for so we call him) was taken sick, so that for some time we did not expect his life. He has never been so well since, though he is comfortable at present. I have myself got a very bad cold and very sore eyes, which makes it very difficult for me to write at all; sometimes I am almost blind.   e

April 17, 1756.—I have written to Miss Prince of Boston to please procure for me the following things: 6 fan mounts, two good ones for ivory sticks, two black and white and two white ones; 1-4 lbs. gum arabic, one large pencil and one short one, one dozen of short cake pans, my milk-pot altered to some shape or other, a pair of coral beads, some cod-fish, patterns of caps, (not ye airy caps for beaux), send me word how to cut ruffles and handkerchiefs, send word how they make gowns. I send by Mr. Burr.

April 19, 1756.—Mr. Burr has set out for Boston. I need not write how lonesome the house and everything about it appears, nor could I if I would. Little Sally observing my gloom upon Mr. Burr's leaving me, sets herself prettily as I think to comfort me. She imagined I was sick. She says, "Mamma, poor Mamma is sick. Don't be sick, Mamma, Papa ain't gone." Upon this I smiled; the little creature's eyes sparkled for joy and she says in transport, "Mamma ain't sick. Dear Mamma," etc.

February 20, 1757.—Mr. Burr was sent for the College about dark, and when he came there he found about twehty young men in one room, crying and begging to know what they should do to be saved. Four of them under the deepest sense of their wicked hearts and need of Christ; Faneuil amongst the rest. How it will rejoice his good mother's heart. Mr. Burr prayed and left them to come home greatly affected. We sat and talked till late and knew not how to lay by the glorious subject.

Feb. 21, 1757.—Good news to write this morning. A minister's son near Philadelphia hopefully received comfort last night in the night. There was little sleep amongst them; some up all night. Mr. Spencer sat up till one o'clock, then left those poor young crea= tures seeking God. The conversion of this young Treat, for that is his name, is a very dear and remarkable one. The particnlars I have not heard, but Mr. Burr says he thinks evidently a work of grace. He has been under some im= pressions for more than a year, but his concern has increased lately.

10 O'clock: A pious young man came from the College for Mr. Burr. He tells me that a great part of the scholars are gathered into one room, crying in great distress, and that another had received comfort. Oh, my heart exults at the thought that God is about to revive religion in general. May we not hope for it? My soul doth magnify the Lord for what he hath done.   ❧   ❧

Eve : The Lord's work goes on gloriously in the College. Mr. Burr sent for Mr. Tennent of Freehold to come and assist in drawing the net ashore, for it is ready to break with the abundance of the fish that are caught in it. Just now he came to the College and is greatly rejoiced.   ❧   ❧   ❧   ❧   ❧

9 O'clock : No work carried on here, but only to get something to eat, and a little of that will suffice too. For my part I haven't any creature to say one word to, and when I am ready to burst, I have recourse to my pen.   ❧   ❧

Mr. Tennent is astonished and amazed, between joy, sorrow, hope and fear, and says he doesn't know what passion is uppermost, but he must call it an angelic joy that he feels, which is the case with us all. My brother is under a great deal of concern among the rest.   e   e   e   e   e   e   e

O what shall I surrender to the Lord for His goodness in pouring out His Spirit in such a wonderful degree!   e

Tuesday, Feb. 25, 1757.—I am ready to set up my Tabernacle and say, "Lord, it is good to be here." Indeed, the thoughts of living have never been so comfortable to me as now. The Lord is indeed here.   e   e   e   e

Wednesday, Aug. 31, 4 o'clock P.M. —Just now I received a letter with a black seal, but it contained blacker news. Gov. Belcher is dead: died this A. M. The righteous are taken away from the evil to come. This is such a loss, that we cannot expect to have made up in a Governor. I feel quite sunk with this and other bad news. His Lordship is returning to New York, and then Halifax will be taken no doubt.

Eve: Mr. Burr not returned. Heavy news Mr. Belcher's death will be to him.   e   e   e   e   e   e   e

Thursday, Eve, Sept. 1, 1757. Mr.

Burr returned in health. O how good is God in preserving him in his goings out and his comings in! These mercies ought not to be forgotten by me.

Mr. Burr, is sent for to preach the Governor's funeral sermon. P. M. : A deal of company.

Friday A. M.—If we go to Boston we shall be there by the second week in October.

Now about Sally and Aaron. Sally has got pretty hearty again, and is not much of a baby; affects to be thought a woman. Nothing she scorns more than to be told she is a child or baby. We are about sending her to school, but Mr. Burr expects she will prove a numb head. But for my part, I think her about middling in all accounts. She grows thinner and more shapeable. I have taken her to meeting and she behaves very well, and can give a good account of what papa does there. She can say some of Dr. Watts' verses by heart and the Lord's Prayer and some other prayers. But she is not over apt about the matter.

Aaron is a little, dirty, noisy boy, very different from Sally almost in everything. He begins to talk a little, is very sly, mischievous, and has more sprightliness than Sally. I must say, he is handsomer, but not so good tempered. He is very resolute, and requires a good governor to bring him to terms.

Princeton, Sept. 2, 1757.

MY dear husband, Mr. Burr, is preparing a funeral discourse in memory of Governor Belcher of Elizabethtown, who died August 31. I have besought him to spare himself the undertaking. To-day he has been getting the sermon ready, and to-morrow he will ride forty miles to deliver it, on the 4th instant, when he should be lying upon a sick bed, and nursed with the greatest care at home. I fear the worst. *   *   *   *

September 5th.—Mr. Burr has returned, but, alas, his fever which was at first of an intermitent kind has settled into one affecting the brain, and he is much of the time in delirium. I have often been alarmed to think God might take him from me. I hope God will help me with His hand, should this awful dispensation come to me. He has an infinite right to His own. *   *

Princeton, Oct. 7, 1757.

MY loss, shall I attempt to describe it? God only can know. What can be written to set forth the affliction of a poor disconsolate widow and two fatherless ones? I have lost all that could be desired in a creature. I have lost all that I ever set my heart on, in this world. In his eulogium, Gov. Livingston said: "Cease not to weep an angel, whom you loved a man." Oh, I am afraid I shall conduct myself so as to bring dishonor to my God, and the religion I profess. No, let me rather die, this moment. I am overcome. To God only will I carry my complaint. I will speak it to His glory, that I think He has in an uncommon degree discovered Himself to be an all-sufficient God, a full fountain of good.

Princeton, Nov. 2, 1757.

I HAVE just written a letter to my affectionate and honored father, in answer to one full of consolation, sent to me by him after Mr. Burr's death. In it I said, and this I wish to put on record as a part of my journal :

"One evening, in talking of the glorious state my dear departed husband must be in, my soul was carried out in such large desires after that glorious state, that I was forced to retire from the family to conceal my joy. When alone, I was so transported, and my soul carried out in such eager desires after perfection and the full enjoyment of God, and to serve Him uninterruptedly, that I think my nature would not have borne much more. I think, that night I had a foretaste of Heaven. The frame continued in some good degree, the whole night. I slept but little, and when I did, my dreams were all of heavenly and divine things. Frequently, since, I have felt the same in kind, though not in degree. I beg leave to add my need of the earnest prayers of my dear and honored parents, and all good people that I may not at last be a castaway; but that God would constantly grant me new supplies of divine grace."   e   e   e   e   e   e

My honored father's letter was so affectionate, comforting and refreshing, that I shall transcribe it in my journal:

Stockbridge, Nov. 20, 1757,

Dear Daughter:

I thank you for your most comfortable letter; but more especially would I thank God, that He has granted you such thoughts to write. How good and kind is your Heavenly Father! How do the bowels of His tender love and compassion appear, while He is correcting you by so great a stroke of His hand! Indeed, He is a faithful God; He will remember His covenant forever; and never will fail them that trust in Him. But don't be surprised, as though some strange thing had happened to you, if after this light, clouds of darkness should return. Perpetual sunshine is not usual in this world, even to God's true saints. But I hope, if God should hide His face in some respect, even this will be in faithfulness to you, to purify you, and fit you for yet further and better light.　　●　　●　　●　　●

As to Lucy's coming home, her mother will greatly need her, especially if we remove in the spring. But yet, whether your circumstances don't much more loudly call for her continuance there, must be left with you and her. She must judge whether she can come consistently with her health and comfort at such a season of the year. If she comes, let her buy me a staff, and after advice, and get a good one or none. Mr. Effelstein has promised her a good horse and side-saddle, and his son to wait on her to Stockbridge; and I suppose Mr. Fonda can let her have a horse and side-saddle to Mr. Effelstein's.

Timmy is considerably better, though yet very weak. We all unite in love to you, Lucy, and your chilhren. Your mother is very willing to leave Lucy's coming away wholly to you and her. I am, your most tender and affectionate father,

Jonathan Edwards.

To Mrs. Esther Burr,
　　at Princeton, New Jersey.

Princeton, N. J. April, 1758.

I HAVE taken this brief memorial of Mr. Edwards, "My most tender and affectionate father;" yes, and alas, my last words from his pen, from the "Boston Gazette" of the 10th instant: "On Wednesday, the twenty-second of March, at Nassau Hall, an eminent servant of God, the reverend, pious, Mr. Jonathan Edwards, President of the College of New Jersey; a gentleman of distinguished abilities and a heavenly temper of mind; a most rational, generous, catholic and exemplary Christian, admired by all who knew him, for his uncommon candour, and disinterested benevolence; a pattern of temperance, meekness, patience, charity; always steady, calm and serene; a very judicious and instructive preacher; and a most exellent divine. And as he lived, cheerfully resigned to the will of Heaven, so he died, or rather, as the Scriptures emphatically express it, with respect to good men, he fell asleep in Jesus, without the least appearance of pain." e e e

I wonder if this tribute to my honored father's memory were not from the pen of the family's kind friend, Rev. Thomas Prince. ❧ ❧ ❧ ❧ ❧

But, I must copy this letter, too, from my dear widowed mother to poor widowed me; yes, and my two fatherless ones:

Stockbridge, April 3, 1758.

My Dear Child:

A holy and a good God has covered us with a dark cloud. O that we may kiss the rod, and lay our hands upon our mouths! The Lord has done it. He has made me adore His goodness, that we have had him so long. But, my God lives and He has my heart. O what a legacy my husband and your father has left us. We are all given to God, and there I am, and love to be. ❧ ❧

Your ever affectionate mother,

Sarah Edwards.

Final Note.

✦ ✦ ✦

ESTHER EDWARDS BURR died April 7, 1758, about eight months after her husband, President Burr of Princeton, sixteen days after her father, President Edwards, President Burr's successor, and about six months before her mother, in the twenty-seventh year of her age, leaving to the mercies of the world, two orphan children, Sally and Aaron, respectively four and two years of age It is said of her in the Life of President Edwards, that " she exceeded most of her sex in the beauty of her person, as well in her behaviour and conversation She discovered an unaffected, natural freedom towards persons of all ranks with whom she conversed She had a lively, sprightly imagination, a quick and penetrating discernment, and a good judgment She possessed an uncommon degree of wit and vivacity, which yet was consistent with pleasantness and good nature, and she knew how to be facetious and sportive, without trespassing on the bounds of decorum, or of strict, serious religion In short, she seemed formed to please, and especially to please one of Mr Burr's taste and character, in whom he was exceedingly happy But, what crowned all her excellencies and was her chief glory was religion She left a number of manuscripts and it was hoped they would be made public but they are now lost "

(-)